Contributory Author
Brian Knapp, BSc, PhD
Art Director
Duncan McCrae, BSc
Special photography
Graham Servante
Editorial consultants
Anna Grayson, Rita Owen
Science advisors
Andrew Burnett, MB.ChB, MRCGP, DRCOG,
Family Doctor
Jack Brettle, BSc, PhD, Chief Research Scientist,
Pilkington plc
Nutritional advisors
Janet McCrae, Elizabeth Mickleson
Environmental Education Advisor
Colin Harris, County Advisor, Herts. CC
Production controller
Gillian Gatehouse
Print consultants
Landmark Production Consultants Ltd
Printed and bound in Hong Kong
Produced by *EARTHSCAPE EDITIONS*

First published in the United Kingdom in 1991
by Atlantic Europe Publishing Company Limited
86 Peppard Road, Sonning Common, Reading,
Berkshire, RG4 9RP, UK
Tel: (0734) 723751   Fax: (0734) 724488

Copyright © 1991
Atlantic Europe Publishing Company Limited

Reprinted in 1992

British Library Cataloguing in Publication Data

Knapp, Brian
    Food
    1. Food – For children
    I. Title   II. Series
    641.3
          ISBN 1-869860-75-6

In this book you will find some words that have been shown in **bold** type. There is a full explanation of each of these words on pages 46 and 47.

On many pages you will find experiments that you might like to try for yourself. They have been put in a coloured box like this.

Acknowledgements
The publishers would like to thank the following:
Leighton Park School, Micklands Primary School,
Redlands County Primary School and Palmer
Park Stadium.

Picture credits
t=top b= bottom l=left r=right

All photographs from the Earthscape Editions
photographic library except the following:
Hutchison Library 36; ZEFA 5, 8, 37, 45

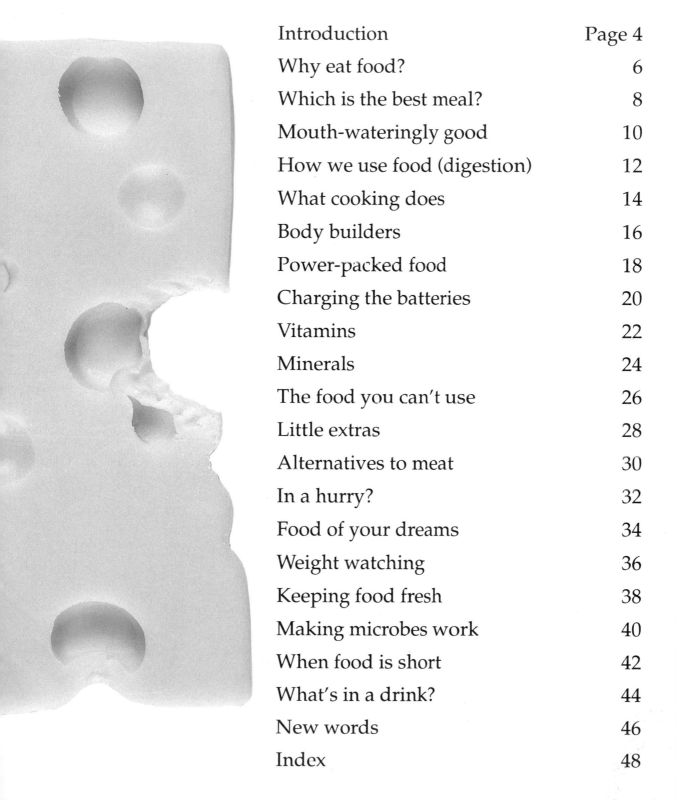

Contents

Introduction

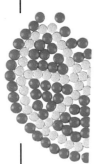

All living things need food to live. Plants are able to make their own food from the soil, from water and from sunshine. Animals get their food by eating plants (they are called **herbivores**) or other animals (in which case they are called **carnivores**). Some, including humans, eat both plants and animals.

Food provides **nutrients**. They are called **proteins**, **carbohydrates**, **fat**, **minerals**, **vitamins** and water. A healthy balanced **diet** needs to contain all six.

Today's world is too crowded to get all the food we need for a balanced diet by hunting wild animals or gathering seeds, roots and fruits from wild plants. Only fishermen still hunt wild animals. Most of our food comes from millions of farms, some just big enough to support a family, others so large they are as big as countries.

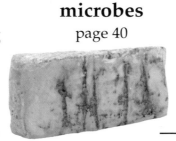

4

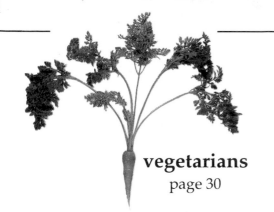

vegetarians
page 30

fat
page 20

x

fibre
page 26

taste
page 10

digestion
page 12

hunger
page 42

People in each part of the world traditionally produce a unique range of foods to eat, and speedy transport means wc can enjoy the foods grown world-wide.

Food chemists (they are called food technologists) can even imitate natural food in their laboratories. They can make food in the way they want, changing the tastes, the colours, the smells and the textures.

So with such variety, are all the things we eat and enjoy good for us? Does it matter what we eat, or how much? Does it make any difference which way we cook our food or for how long? Do people in other countries eat better or worse than us?

To find out about the fascinating world of food, just turn to the page of your choice and begin your discoveries.

proteins
page 16

drinks
page 44

fast food
page 32

meals
page 8

weight
page 36

Why eat food?

There seem to be so many kinds of food available that will keep us healthy. How does the body make use of the foods we eat? How does it extract the **energy** we need to keep us going? You only know the answers to these questions when you know what we are made of.

Sweet potato, the root of a plant

People: backwards plants

Plants use the energy of the Sun to build their tissues. It's a process called **photosynthesis.** In this way some of the Sun's energy gets locked inside plants.

When people and animals eat plants they release and make use of the energy that the plants have stored.

People are not able to use all parts of a plant as food. We do not have the right chemicals in our digestive system to release this energy. Herbivores (like rabbits and cattle) are able to **digest** all plant material. In turn we are able to digest animal meat. It is known as a **food chain**.

Caterpillars

Mango fruit

Pineapple, fruit
of a plant

What's needed

The body works like a chemical factory, changing the raw materials called food into the nutrients that give us energy and build new body **cells**.

No one food contains all the nutrients we need, so we have to eat a variety of foods. We also have to be careful about the amount of food we eat. Too much and we start to get fat, and too little and we can become ill. The right amount of the foods we need is called a balanced diet.

Crab

Whelk taken
from its shell

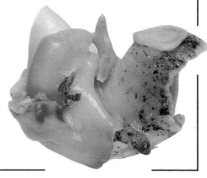

Which is the best meal?

Which would you choose as the most healthy meal? A steak, vegetables and pudding, a meal of maize flour, bananas and berries, or a meal of fish, rice and spices?

Whichever one you choose can give the good – nutritious – food you need because no one type of food is better than any other.

Some or all?
Many foods provide a balanced meal. Trying out new foods can not only be interesting and fun, but it can help you to see how a balanced meal is made.

The rule, however, is: don't just eat some parts of a meal, all the parts are needed for a balanced diet.

Find out what's in food
It is very difficult to find out what is inside food because most foods contain so many nutrients mixed up. Many processed or prepared foods now have the contents – called the **ingredients** – on the side of the pack.

Look at a selection of packs to find out what is in each food.

A table laden with many kinds of food for a Thanksgiving Festival. It is easy to choose both a balanced meal or an unhealthy meal from such a delicious selection

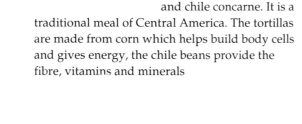

These are steamed bananas wrapped up in a banana leaf. It is a traditional meal of central Africa. Along with corn (maize) it makes a **staple** diet for millions of people. Bananas are high in fat for energy as well as fibre, vitamins and minerals

This meal consists of tortillas and chile concarne. It is a traditional meal of Central America. The tortillas are made from corn which helps build body cells and gives energy, the chile beans provide the fibre, vitamins and minerals

When experience counts

Most traditional meals in the world provide a balanced diet. This is because people have worked out by experience what is best for them. It is all a matter of choice and tradition.

This meal contains a slice of lamb, fried potatoes and peas. Lamb contains the protein which helps to build cells and the fat stores energy, potatoes provide more energy and peas give special ingredients such as **fibre**, vitamins and minerals. It is a traditional meal of Europe, Australasia and North America

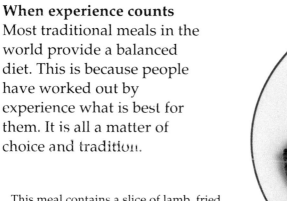

This meal consists of rice, fish and a wide variety of vegetables. The green slices on the top are peppers. Fish provides the protein and fat, rice gives energy and the vegetables give the fibre, vitamins and minerals. It is a traditional dish of South East Asia

Mouth-wateringly good

Think about the food you would most like to eat. You don't need to look at it or even smell it – just think about it.

As you are thinking notice how your mouth begins to water, to produce the fluids called **saliva**. Special **glands** at the sides of your mouth have been switched on by the brain. They are preparing themselves to help the food go down.

Tastes good

Taste is a way of finding out what food is like. You can look at it, feel it and even smell it, but the final test is always what it tastes like.

Your tongue has special tasting spots called taste buds. Here there are sensitive cells that can tell whether food is sweet, sour, salty or bitter.

What are mouth juices?

Saliva is a mixture of chemicals designed to act as a superfast means of breaking down foods. When your brain sends messages of hunger, it also switches on the glands that produce saliva.

If you sometimes don't feel like eating it is because the brain is not sending the right signals.

Enjoying your food depends on wanting to eat.

Taste bud test
Where exactly are the taste buds for saltiness, sweetness, sourness and bitterness? Test your tongue with drops of salt water, sugar water, vinegar and strong, cold tea.

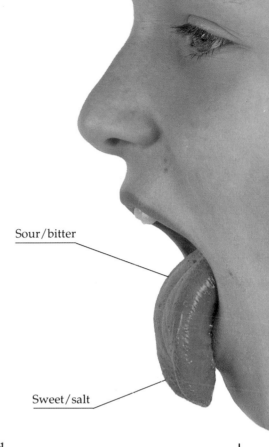

Sour/bitter

Sweet/salt

Food tastes to check
 The taste buds are clumped together. They are found in the cracks on the surface of your tongue.

At the front of your tongue are taste buds which check food and drink for saltiness. Too much salt is harmful.

There are taste buds here too which check the food for sweetness – sugar tells you the food could be high in energy.

At the back of the tongue are taste buds for sourness and bitterness – two tastes that may indicate that the food is poisonous or has gone bad.

Follow the food
As soon as you eat some food your body begins to digest it. You can actually follow its path by listening carefully to your body. The stethoscope shown here is a medical instrument for listening inside a body. By placing it against your jaw you can hear sounds of chewing, by placing it on your throat you can hear swallowing and by placing it on your stomach you can hear the food being churned round and round. Then find out what really happens on the next page.

How we use food

All food is a mixture of useful things and those that have no food value to us.

To get the best from the food we eat, our body takes out the good things and lets the useless ones pass through. This is called digestion.

Vital stages
To give you some idea of what each part of the digestive system does, these pictures show various forms of carrot treated to represent the way the system works and what the products look like.

2/ Stomach's cauldron
In the stomach there are 25 million minute glands that pump out up to two and a half litres of digestive (called **gastric**) juices a day – most of it a form of powerful hydrochloric acid.

Even this fearsome brew needs time to do its work thoroughly. So food remains in the stomach for several hours.

3/ Straining gut
When the digested brew leaves the stomach it goes on a long journey – some three metres – through a long coiled and twisted tube called our gut, or intestine. Here the nutrients are taken out through the tube walls. The nutrients are carried in the blood to the thousand billion cells that need them.

1/ Crushing teeth

The food we eat needs to be turned from lumps into smaller pieces, so that the body's digestive chemicals can get to work on it.

Your front teeth – the incisors – rip the food apart and cut it into bite-sized pieces. The back ones – the molars – are broad and flat and are designed to crush and flatten the food.

4/ When all is done

What is left is waste, mainly a stringy substance called fibre, and liquid, mainly water.

This slowly makes its way to the end of the gut where it gets pressed together so it can easily be got rid of when we visit the toilet.

What cooking does

Cooking tenderises food by heating it.
People have baked, steamed and boiled their food from earliest times. In the **Stone Age**, corn was ground with water and the paste dropped onto hot stones to make bread.

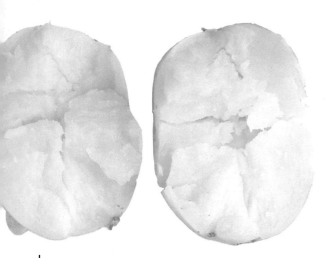

Cooking temperatures
Cooking tenderises and sterilises food, killing the many harmful **microbes** that could cause illness.

To make sure cooking has killed the harmful microbes it is best to bring the food to at least boiling point for several minutes.

Roasting and frying work at a much higher temperature than boiling and harmful microbes are killed within a few seconds. But only just warming food can be dangerous because it helps harmful microbes to breed.

Bursting out
Try eating a piece of raw potato. What does it taste like? Is it easy to digest?

The trouble is from the **starch** that makes up a fifth of the potatoe's weight. When you cook a potato it makes the starch swell and the cells burst open. This makes the potato easier to digest.

Boiling and steaming

Many seeds have dried out before they have been harvested. All the goodness is firmly locked within them. If they were eaten raw much of the seed would pass right through our bodies before there was time to extract the nutrients.

By soaking in hot water, or boiling, the seeds take on water, swell, and become more tender. In this form they can be digested more readily.

Roasting

Roasting is used for fatty foods. Many types of meat are tough and hard to break up when raw. Our teeth cannot bite or crush raw meat and so it cannot properly be prepared for the stomach.

When meat, such as the lamb shown in this picture, is roasted the fats begin to melt inside the meat and the cell walls become less tough.

Body builders

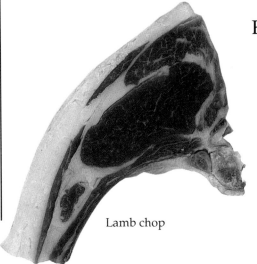

Lamb chop

Every food has its special qualities. On the next few pages you will find out how some of these work and how they help us to keep healthy.

If you look at a body builder's muscles you might think that muscles were made by exercise. However, the main body builders are actually the substances that make up your cells – proteins. A body builder simply has all the individual muscle cells swollen.

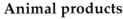

Hard cheese

Animal products

Animal products such as meat, fish, eggs and milk are concentrated food. People who do a lot of training for sports events often eat large amounts of these foods to help build the size of the muscle cells in their bodies.

As young people grow they also need large amounts of protein to help increase the number of body cells. Eating animal products is one way of providing this.

Red Snapper

Peanut butter

Peanuts

Peanut butter
Proteins can be found concentrated in plant foods. Cereals, such as rice or oats contain protein, although it is not as concentrated as in animal products.

One source of concentrated plant protein is peanuts. Eaten either whole or made into peanut butter they are good body builders.

Watch proteins appear
Break an egg into a frying pan with a little fat and begin to fry it. At first the 'white' of the egg is colourless. It is packed with protein but you cannot see it.

As the egg fries the protein changes colour and the white of the egg appears.

Eggs

Power-packed food

Sugar is the main source of instant energy. To get this we can eat foods that have sugars bound up in them. They are called carbohydrates. Then, when they are needed, the body can break down these substances and turn them into the sugars we need for energy.

Fudge bar: there is as much energy locked up in this bar as there is in a stick of dynamite

Sugar for stamina

Some athletes use a kind of sugar called glucose to give them extra energy when they are training hard.

If you take sugar this way the body does not have to digest food to make the sugars but they can be taken into the blood and into the muscles swiftly.

Not all types of sugar work this way. You can't get a surge of energy from simply sucking an ordinary sweet.

Baked potatoes

Surprising sugars

A potato, a handful of rice or a slice of bread are each good sources of carbohydrates for giving you long-term energy. They may not taste very sweet, but that is because the energy is locked up in another form of carbohydrate called starch.

What does starch look like?

It is easy to see the starch in some foods. Try doing one or more of these investigations.

Cut a raw potato into several pieces on a chopping board. The whitish milky liquid that oozes out is starch.

Make a dough out of flour and water, then make the dough really wet and wring it out over a cup. The milky liquid in the cup is also starch.

Put some rice in a saucepan and boil it. Then pour the excess water away into a cup. Again, the milky liquid contains lots of starch.

Boiled rice

Sugary dangers

As sugars are so important our bodies do not like to give any of them up readily. They keep the excess stored away in case of need. The body's way of storing things is to produce fat. This is one of the reasons people who eat lots of sugar tend to get fat.

A sugar coating over your teeth and gums gives harmful microbes plenty of food to live on. As they use up the sugar they produce a sticky acid substance that is called **plaque**, which rots your teeth. This girl's teeth have been painted with a special dentist's dye which shows blue wherever there is plaque.

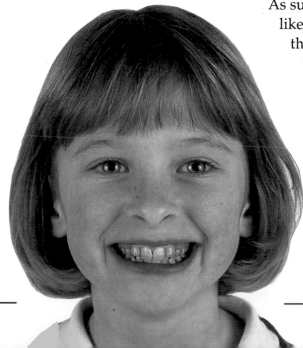

Charging the batteries

Fat is really packed with energy. Sometimes the fat is easy to see. If you look at a piece of meat you will see that it has a kind of marbling over it. These white streaks are fat. They give the animal's muscles extra energy whenever it needs it – such as to run away from attack.

We all have fatty marbling in our muscles and some grown ups have excess fat in some less welcome places!

Look for the fat
You can find fat in all kinds of foods, both from animals and plants. When you eat your meals look to see how fatty the foods are. Perhaps they have been cooked in fat?

Look for the marbling in meat. Where else do animals keep their fat? Would it be easy to cut away so that you ate less animal fat?

Many foods give out fat during cooking. See how much fat is left in a frying pan after different foods have been cooked.

Overcharged batteries
People's need for food has changed little this century. However, people in better off countries now eat far more fat than they used to, or than the body needs. And it shows! In young people too much fat may contribute to skin spots; in older people it forms into loose folds of flesh.

Fat globules on the surface of a **stock** soup

An avocado is a green fruit which is very high in fat as well as protein

How does fat move?

Our bodies use the fats from plants and animals to make the kinds of fats our bodies need. The fats are then carried to all parts of our bodies in our blood.

As people get older their bodies are not as good at handling the fatty substances made from animals as when they were young, and some of it gets 'parked' on the walls of blood vessels. If this gets too thick it can cause a 'traffic jam' and block up the flow of blood: it is one cause of heart attacks.

To lessen the risk of heart attack many people choose to eat fat made from plants because this is thought to be less dangerous.

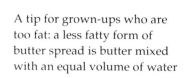

A tip for grown-ups who are too fat: a less fatty form of butter spread is butter mixed with an equal volume of water

21

Vitamins

The main foods we eat are proteins (to build the cells of our bodies), fat and sugars to give us energy. But they are not quite enough. We also need small amounts of some rather special chemicals called vitamins.

It is possible, but not as nice and quite unnecessary, to provide many of vitamins you need by eating vitamin pills

What do vitamins do?

Vitamins are chemicals that help the system work well. They are especially important in helping the body's defence systems fight off illness.

Vitamins A, B and C are found in foods, especially fruit and cereals.

Vitamin D is different. It is mostly made by the body in the skin using sunlight, although it is also found in milk.

Limeys cure scurvy

In the past sailors on long voyages used to suffer from a mysterious illness called scurvy. It sometimes killed most of the sailors on ships.

Scurvy is a disease caused by not getting enough vitamin C. Sailors did not take any fresh fruit with them on their voyages and so they gradually got more and more ill.

In the nineteenth century British ships were all made to carry limes (their name for the fruit we now call lemons) on board to keep scurvy at bay. This is, incidentally, how British people got their world-wide nickname 'limey'.

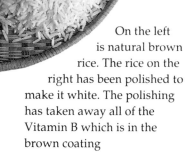

On the left is natural brown rice. The rice on the right has been polished to make it white. The polishing has taken away all of the Vitamin B which is in the brown coating

Grapes: filled with Vitamin C

Vitamins vitamins

Look on the side of packets and cans to see which vitamins the food contains.

Many packets tell you how much you need each day. Find out if you get enough just from processed foods.

Boiled out

It is easy to lose some of the goodness in food as you prepare it. For example, many skins are high in vitamin C. Peeling apples and potatoes, for example, loses much of the goodness. Boiling vegetables also carries away many of the vitamins.

To see that boiling has some effect, boil some dark greens, such as spinach, in a saucepan. Drain off the greens, but carefully keep the water they were boiled in. The water will be green in colour, showing that some of the vegetable has been dissolved out.

The goodness in the liquid can be made into a soup or a sauce.

Minerals

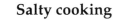

Some of the most vital chemicals in your body occur in very small amounts. For example, you can't build body cells without minute traces of substances called minerals. These are things like calcium (as in chalk), sodium (from salt), potassium, iron (which gives blood its red colour), and iodine.

Fortunately, we don't have to seek out these minerals. Most of them come naturally in some very common foods.

Calcium bound up in milk is a lot easier to digest than a stick of chalk – also made from calcium

Salty cooking

Salt is one of the most important minerals because the body uses it to help extract nutrients through the walls of the gut.

Most foods contain the vital sodium in salt, and most food is cooked in salty water to bring out the flavour, so adding even more salt to your food is not necessary except in hot climates. Too little salt will, however, make you feel weary and you will find it hard to move about.

Excess salt can be bad for you because of the way it makes the body try to dilute it. The heart pumps faster to try to get rid of the salt and this causes your blood pressure to rise.

Salt

Salt is a common mineral that we need in our food. People in hot climates need a lot more salt than those who live in cool places because it is lost as we sweat. If you lick the back of your arm after you have got hot you may notice how salty it tastes.

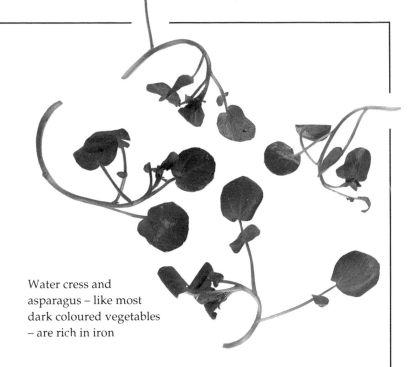

Water cress and asparagus – like most dark coloured vegetables – are rich in iron

Why minerals are added

Although they are needed in tiny quantities, minerals are vital to our diet and without them we can become prone to many health problems.

Some minerals are added to all the food we eat. In many countries, for example, it is common to add iodine to the salt. It does not show or taste, but iodine is vital to prevent the appearance of unpleasant throat swelling called goitres which used to be common.

Fluoride is another mineral which is added to water or toothpaste to help give teeth that resist decay.

Curry powder is very rich in iron

The food you can't use

A large part of your food can't be directly used by your body. It is called fibre. Fibre is a carrier for all the good things that your body can use.

Fibre may sound like stringy plants, but it is often found in the most unlikely places. Even the soft fleshy parts of most fruits have lots of fibre.

Bananas are high in fibre

Bread and other cereals provide the main source of fibre for most people

Get it carried away
If you don't have a lot of fibre in your food, the wastes may stay inside you for longer than is good. You won't find fibre in meat, so it's important to have lots of vegetables, grains and fruits to help your food along.

What fibres do
The fibre in your gut is like a broom, sweeping out all the wastes along with it.

Some sorts of fibre – such as the fibre in oats – actually dissolve. They can be particularly good for us because they get into the blood and help to sweep up any excess fats.

Beans appear soft, but they are high in fibre

Where to find fibre

Plants are made of two kinds of materials: soft cells that make up the fleshy parts of the plant; and hard cells that provide the support. The hard and tough cells are called fibre. Sometimes it is easy to see the supporting fibres: they make up the bark on trees and the veins in leaves. But in many cases they are harder to find. An apple, for example, has a lot of tough fibre, but it is mixed in with the soft tissue.

Sometimes you can see the fibres, such as in this celery

Find the fibre

If you boil up some stems of plants and then strain away the hot water you will find the main tough fibres can be separated out more easily.

Little extras

Much of the food we eat may have
something added. Many are the
extracts of plants. We might add a
spice such as pepper at the table, or a
herb such as basil to a soup. Spices and
herbs do a wide range of jobs, some
useful, some just for show.

Basil (herb)

Cardamom
seeds

Spices of life
Spices are the fruits or vegetables of some plants that
are used as natural flavourings and preservatives.
In the past, when food was not as good as it is
today, wealthy people were able to make the food
taste better by using spices. In some cases spices
were also thought to be good for health.
Many spices contain concentrated
minerals and vitamins and help to
give a balanced diet.

Star Anise

Cloves

Nutmeg

Coriander

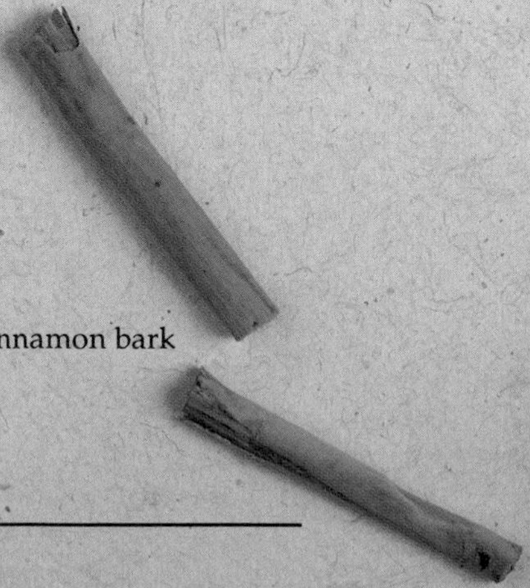

Cinnamon bark

Raw root ginger
and ground ginger

Herbs

Herbs are the leaves of
plants. Some add flavour
to a food, others add both
flavour and scent. Many
forms of China tea use
flavoured and scented herbs.

Oregano (herb)

The spice trade

Most spices come from tropical
plants and in the past a huge trade
developed just to carry spice. One
group of islands (now partly
Indonesia) were called the Spice
Islands and many Europeans grew
wealthy on the Spice Trade.

Garlic

Black pepper corns

Raw and dried chilly
peppers

Alternatives to meat

Meat is not essential for a healthy well balanced diet because proteins, fats and sugars can all be found in plants.

Many people in the world eat a diet made up of mainly or even only of plants. They are called vegetarians.

There are many good ways of getting a balanced and interesting diet without eating meat at all. Here are some of them.

Carrot

How to replace meat
People can get their proteins by eating cereals, beans and nuts. Soya flour – ground up seeds of the soya bean plant – is one of the most nutritious forms of protein and costs much less than meat.

Milk, cheese and eggs are also a good way of getting the same food value as meat.

Pinto bean

Butter bean

Black bean

Black-eyed bean

Haricot bean

Kidney bean

Cheese, full of protein
Hard cheese is one of the most concentrated of common foods.

One hundred grams of cheese contains about a third of all the protein and fat that a person needs each day. It also contains a wide variety of other essential vitamins and minerals. It makes a good substitute for meat in a vegetarian diet.

A dish without meat called a Rogan Josh. It is a mixture of a wide variety of appetising vegetables eaten with rice

Natural vegetables

Fruit and vegetables grown without help from man-made chemicals (often called 'organic' food) do not put on as much weight as those grown by modern methods and so are more expensive to produce.

So whether you eat natural foods or not as part of a vegetarian diet depends on two things: do you have a big enough garden to grow your own food, or are you rich enough to pay for food to be grown without chemicals?

In countries where many people are vegetarians there is usually a very wide variety of plants to choose from. The picture above right shows baskets in an Indonesian market filled with tomatoes and peppers. The picture below it shows part of an Indian market

In a hurry?

For many years eating was a family affair, with everyone eating together at a dinner table. However, today's way of living means that we may often eat separately.

It is less convenient to cook full meals for a variety of people. To match up with this problem many people buy meals that are quick to eat.

Complete meals can be bought already prepared and which simply need to be heated through. They are called fast foods or convenience foods.

Snacks

Snacks that have been made in a factory are not meant to be proper meals. Examples are chocolate bars and crisps. They are meant to keep you going between meals.

Many snacks are high in sugar to give you instant energy, they have lots of fat to make them taste moist and salt to preserve them.

Sugar, fat and salt are not good for you in large amounts. Snacks are fine, but only if they make up a small part of your daily diet.

Fried fish in batter balls is a favourite fast food in South East Asia. Here you see it being cooked at the roadside

French fries is the name given to deep pan-fried potato strips. The potato contains starch for energy, but frying gives them a very high fat content

World of the hamburger

The hamburger is probably the world's favourite fast food.

Hamburgers are easy to eat because frying at a high temperature changes the meat and makes it more tender. This makes it easier to chew and swallow.

A hamburger with all the trimmings can be a balanced meal. Here's why.

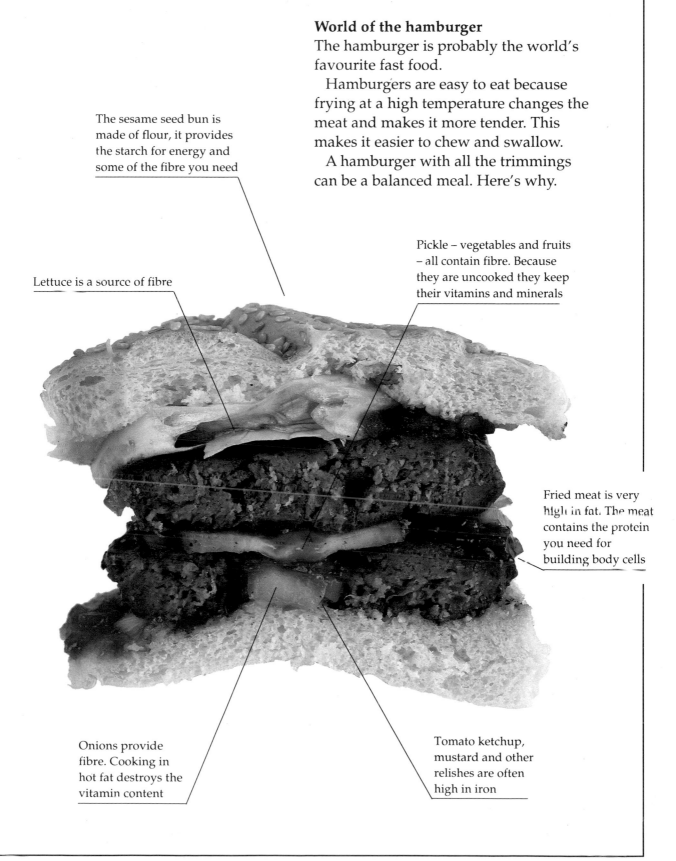

The sesame seed bun is made of flour, it provides the starch for energy and some of the fibre you need

Lettuce is a source of fibre

Pickle – vegetables and fruits – all contain fibre. Because they are uncooked they keep their vitamins and minerals

Fried meat is very high in fat. The meat contains the protein you need for building body cells

Onions provide fibre. Cooking in hot fat destroys the vitamin content

Tomato ketchup, mustard and other relishes are often high in iron

Food of your dreams

Wouldn't it be nice if you could get all your favourite flavours into one food?

This is what many food processing companies try to do. They have a very difficult task. Here are some of the 'tricks of the trade'.

What is the problem?

Food made in a factory has to be made in large amounts, yet is has to look and taste appetising. It must also keep fresh in a shop for days or weeks until it is bought.

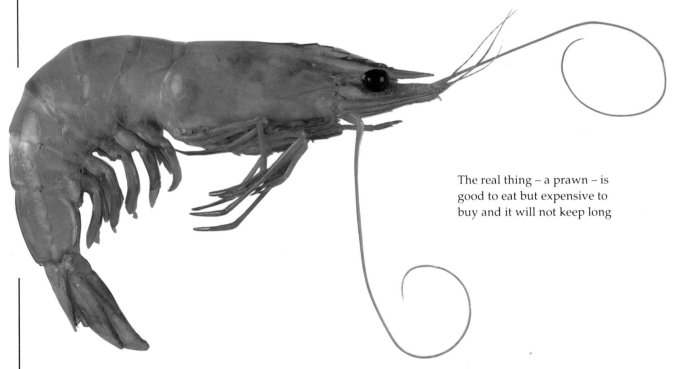

The real thing – a prawn – is good to eat but expensive to buy and it will not keep long

Soft and moist

To give foods their soft, moist taste food makers often use fat instead of water.

Food that contains a large amount of water will soon feel wet and 'soggy'. Fat will keep for many weeks or months without making the food feel wet.

The prawn-flavoured crackers have a flavour like a prawn but the wheat and maize flour used to make the cracker will keep well for months. The prawn-like colour is added after the crackers have been cooked

Copying taste and looks

Flavours are chemicals that are recognised by the taste buds on our tongues. Scientists have to find out what makes up natural tastes and then put a copy of the 'taste' chemicals in the food.

Salt is a natural flavour-boosting chemical which also preserves food. Monosodium glutomate is the name of the most common flavour booster used in the factory.

Colours can also be made in the laboratory and added to new foods to make them look better.

These bottles contain flavours that have been made in the laboratory. Can you guess which one is smelly cheese, which one roast chicken and which is smoky bacon flavour? All these flavours are made artificially without any help from the cheese, chicken or bacon!

Food on a line

Many snacks are really long tubes of food. This shape is easy to make in a machine. The food is cooked at very high temperatures and then squeezed through a hole. The hole can be any shape, and it decides what the final shape of the food will be.

As it comes out of the hole the cooked food swells up and forms a long sausage. Then it goes on to a long moving conveyor belt and it cools.

When the 'sausage' is cool enough it is chopped up into the right lengths and any coatings, like chocolate are poured on. All that remains is a plastic wrapper to keep the harmful microbes at bay and it is ready for the shops.

35

Weight watching

These Mongolian children are fatter than most children of their age. This is because Mongolians believe chubby-looking babies are thought to look beautiful. An extra layer of fat also helps to keep the winter cold at bay. As a result babies tend to look over-fed

Many grown-ups talk about 'watching their weight'. They are concerned that they do not become overweight and their surplus fat begin to show.

One way to keep a check on weight is to find out how much energy is in the food you eat and compare it with how much food scientists believe people need.

Keep an energy diary

Everything you do uses energy. You use this amount of energy each minute when you are: sleeping 1 unit; sitting 1.5 units; walking 4 units; cycling 5 units; playing a sport such as basketball 6 units; swimming 8 units; running fast 11 units.

For example, over nine hours sleep you use 540 units. An average person working in the home or office uses about 2400 units a day.

Make a list of how long you do each type of activity, then add them all up. This tells you how much energy you need to replace.

Ask a grown up to keep a diary as well. They should need about the same number of energy units as you unless they do a very active job.

Use the information on the side of packets and jars or in cookery books to find out how many energy units you have eaten in your food.

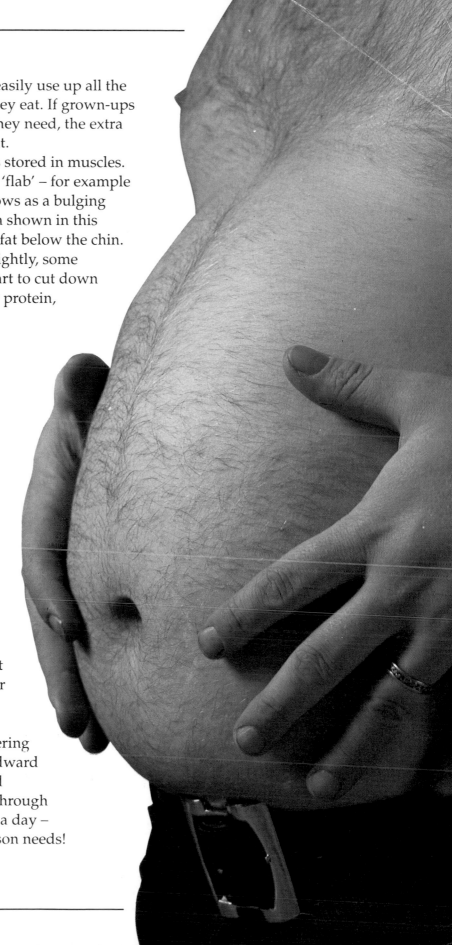

Look for the flab

Most young people easily use up all the energy in the food they eat. If grown-ups eat more food than they need, the extra energy is stored as fat.

The first extra fat is stored in muscles. But any more makes 'flab' – for example a band of fat that shows as a bulging stomach like the man shown in this picture – or hanging fat below the chin.

Because flab is unsightly, some flabby grown-ups start to cut down their food, especially protein, sugar and fat.

Measuring energy

The amount of energy in food is measured in units. In some countries they are called kilojoules or calories.

Over the top

Some people have an illness that makes them eat and eat. A few of these sufferers eat over 20 000 energy units a day. They eat continually through all their waking hours.

The record for eating by someone who was not suffering from a disease is held by Edward Abraham Miller of Oakland California. He ate his way through 25 000 energy units of food a day – ten times the amount a person needs!

Keeping food fresh

Harmful microbes lurk in all our food. Mostly they do no harm. But when they multiply quickly they break down the food in special ways that release poisons.

If we eat too many live harmful microbes they can play havoc with our bodies and make us very ill. So keeping food fresh means keeping the harmful microbes at bay. There are lots of ways to do this – the best of all is to eat food while it is fresh.

A frozen pizza

Cold and out

Harmful microbes need warm conditions for rapid growth. A fridge dramatically slows the growth of harmful microbes but it doesn't stop it.

Freezing food stops the harmful microbes growing almost completely. They don't die when they are frozen, but they don't multiply much either. This is why you can safely keep food in a freezer for many months before you need to eat it.

Salt and sugar (in the form of honey) are the world's oldest preservatives. Rubbing salt into meat and fish locks up the water inside a food so that microbes cannot make use of it. Heating fruit with honey or sugar to make jam has the same effect

Dried caterpillar

Dried out

Harmful microbes need water to survive. One way of preserving food is to dry it out completely.

Freeze-dried coffee and soups are common forms of dried foods. When the food is needed for eating it is simply mixed with boiling water.

New techniques have made this method much better. Most instant coffee, instant soup and instant powdered meals are freeze dried, and they will take up water again in seconds.

Canned sardines

Canned safe

Canned food is cooked to kill off the harmful microbes. Then it is sealed with a lid.

Food that was put in cans over a century ago is still fresh and can be eaten.

Preserving food is most important in hot countries Nearly all the food in this shop is dried, pickled, or canned

Food can be kept in jars and then steeped in vegetable acids. This is called pickling. Microbes cannot multiply easily in acid conditions. Vinegar and lemon juice are two common vegetable acids

Making microbes work

Cheese: food from microbes
Cheese is one of the oldest and most nutritious foods. It is made from milk using a microbe called rennet.

Milk is warmed and then mixed with the rennet. After some hours the milk separates out and the soft cheese (called the curd) can be taken away in a fine meshed cloth.

The ripening process may take many months and it is usually done in cool places. During this time more microbes break down the curd into hard cheese.

Microbes have been used by cooks for thousands of years. They are used to make bread, butter, cheese, yoghurt, beer and many other fine foods. The trick is in using the right microbes and controlling the way they work.

There are many blue cheeses. The blue or green colour is made by a special mould that grows on the cheese. It is quite harmless

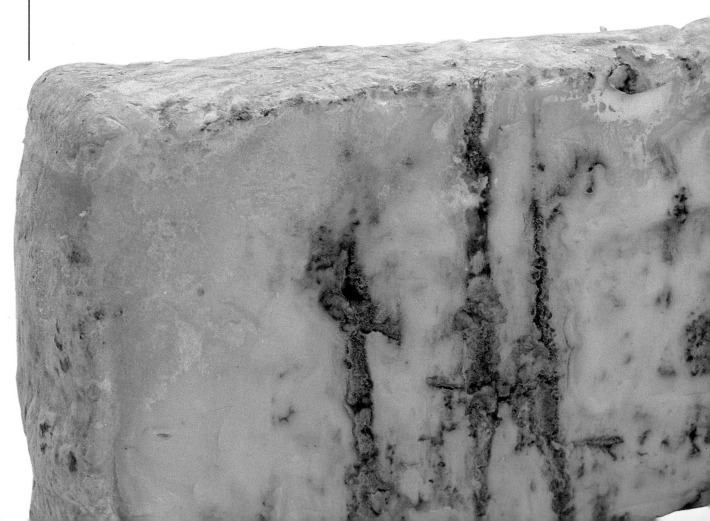

Make your own yoghurt

Yoghurt is a smooth, slightly sour and creamy food that can be made from milk using microbes.

The easiest way to get more yoghurt is to use some of the microbes in yoghurt you buy from a shop. You might like to ask a grown-up to help you.

Take 4 tablespoons of shop yoghurt and let it stand in a warm room for about 3 hours.

Bring a litre of milk to the boil, let it cool slightly then add the yoghurt. Put the bowl with the yoghurt over a saucepan with water and keep the water hot but not boiling.

After two or three hours it will have gone to a creamy liquid like custard. Now you can put it in the fridge. When cold serve as a dessert.

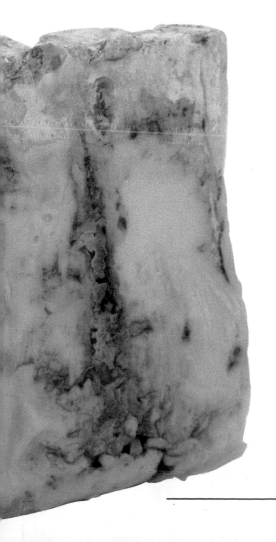

Caution:
Be careful with boiling water

Bread

If you make bread from flour, water and salt it is flat and lifeless. The fresh, light and airy bread that is normally baked relies on a microbe to do the work. It is called yeast.

Yeast is added to the dough mixture and then kneaded (push and pulled). This allows the microbes to get to work. When the dough is put into an oven and baked the yeast is killed.

When food is short

We take our food for granted. We expect to be well fed every day. But over half the world is not so lucky.

Many people get one proper meal at most. Many find they have to go whole days without food.

When people go without food the body tries to call on its own reserves. This can eventually make people very ill.

If you don't eat

If somebody stops eating the body calls on the supplies of food it has stored against emergencies.

The fat reserves in the body are used first. As a result a person becomes noticably thinner.

If a person doesn't eat for several days their body also tries to make the best use of the fats it has left. As a result it is impossible to work normally. Instead they become more tired and weaker.

People who have not eaten for a long time, and people who go on a severe diet, find it difficult to do anything quickly because the body is working so slowly.

When food is short people tend to turn to cheaper and less nutritious foods.

In Africa, for example, a root called cassava is grown as an emergency crop when there is a drought. The cassava plant is not rich in nutriment

Poor workers

Many people in poor countries cannot work very hard. This is not because they are lazy but because they eat too little food to give them the energy they need for hard work.

The best way to get good work is to make sure the workers are properly fed.

These young Samburu boys are thin to our eyes because they do not have a lot of extra fat in their muscles

Charity workers giving extra food to women with babies and small children to ensure they remain healthy.

Each woman keeps a chart of her children's weight to make sure they are not undernourished

Famines

Famines are times when a country runs short of food. This may be because of war or because a harvest has failed.

In a famine thousands of people will have to go without food. Soon they will become too weak to help themselves and they can easily die. This is why it is so important to get food to famine areas as quickly as possible.

What's in a drink?

Most people don't think of drinks as food. But they are as important to our bodies as any solid food.

Liquids do many valuable things, from replacing the water that we lose by sweating and breathing, helping to make new blood cells to making sure that waste products get flushed from our systems.

Drinking water contains many minerals in solution. Often there will be calcium, iron, and minute traces of many others that are essential to health

Living on drink

Even water contains many valuable nutrients. Because they are dissolved in the water we cannot see them, but this air plant shows how useful they can be. The plant gets all its food from dissolved materials that come with the rainwater.

Sometimes, when people are ill and they cannot take solid food, water mixed with sugar and salt can provide enough essential foods until they are well enough to take solids.

A bromeliad

Magic milk

Half a litre of milk a day will give you all the calcium you need and much more. Milk contains vitamins A, B and D. The fat in milk will also give you lots of long-term energy.

The type of milk called semi-skimmed milk has most of the fat taken away, but the calcium is still there, so it's good news for those who might get too fat.

Skimmed milk does *not* have vital the vitamins, so it is best avoided by young people.

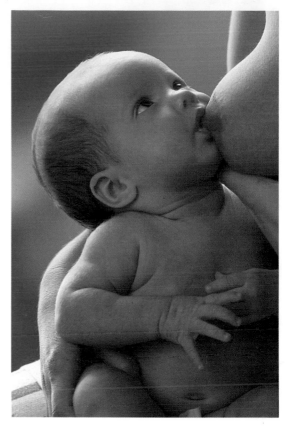

Food for the young

The time when people need the most care with their food is when they are very young. Mother's milk is very high in all the foods needed to make a baby grow healthily.

Babies get their mother's milk by breast feeding. This supply of liquids is vital for healthy growth.

Some people, especially in poor countries, think that because they have to buy dried milk it must be better than mother's milk. This is completely wrong. Ordinary dried milk has had much of the goodness taken out of it and it was never meant for babies.

As a result of this mistake many children grow up weak even though their mothers have done what they thought was best. It shows clearly why it is important to understand about food.

A bottled or canned drink usually contains dissolved sugar as well as colourings, flavourings and preservatives. Most of these drinks help give instant energy

45

New words

carbohydrate
a group of substances that includes a number of sugar-making chemicals, of which the most important is starch

carnivore
an animal, such as a tiger or a bear, that gets all of its food needs from eating other animals

cells
the basic building blocks from which the body is made. Our cells are constantly being renewed and for this the body needs protein

diet
the types of food we eat. When people speak of 'going on a diet', they usually mean they are going to change their diet to one with less energy in it

digest
the way in which the body breaks down the food into useful chemicals

energy
the power in food locked away as chemicals. We release the energy during digestion

fat
the substance that the body makes to store energy

fibre
the materials that are found in plants but which are indigestible

food chain
the many animals and plants that live together in a balance, each dependent on the other in some way

gastric juices
the chemicals the body makes in order to break down the food we eat

glands
a group of cells which have become specialised for the purpose of producing some special chemical made from parts of the blood, for example the saliva glands

herbivore
an animal, such as a cow, a rabbit or an elephant, that gets all of its food needs from plants. People are not herbivores because they can choose to eat meat or plants. People fall into the group called omnivores

ingredients
the foods that go to make up a mixture. The ingredients of a cake, for example, may be flour, water, fat, salt and cherries

microbes
a general term used in this book for all microscopic organisms that may cause harm if they are left to multiply in food

minerals
naturally occurring substances of the Earth, such as chalk and iron, that plants and animals absorb and use to build their tissues

nutrients
essential materials that the body needs to make more cells. Nutrients include calcium (from milk), salt and iron (from dark-coloured vegetables)

photosynthesis
the process that plants use to make new cells from sunlight, water, air and minerals in the soil

plaque
a substance produced in the mouth. It is a sticky acid substance that makes the food for bacteria. At the same time as eating the plaque, the bacteria eat into the surface of the teeth causing tooth decay. Toothpaste contains substances which balance out the acid and stop bacteria from feeding

protein
the name given to substances that make the walls of the bodies cells. Young people need to eat a large amount of protein otherwise their growth might be stunted

saliva
the chemicals that are used to start the digestion of food

staple
foods that are essential to healthy living. Staples include grains such as wheat, maize and rice

starch
one of the common substances in the carbohydrate group. Starches are our most common form of day to day energy

stock
a liquid made from boiling animal products such as bones with vegetable remains to get the remaining goodness from them

Stone Age
the earliest time of civilisation, over 3000 years ago, when people mainly used stone implements

vitamins
essential chemicals that the body uses to help prevent illness and in many other essential processes, They are easily destroyed by cooking or storing food. This is why fresh food is so essential

Index